HOW TO IMPROVE YOUR LANGUAGE SKILLS & SPEAK EFFECTIVELY!

Preeti G
English Language Trainer

Published by

Amazon

For Aadit, Ahaana, Himanshu & Mom!

Introduction

No one gets better at something overnight!

And, who better to speak about it than **Myself** (Yes, you heard that right!)

As someone who was struggling to restart her career in her early 40s, by pursuing her childhood passion - learning a foreign language, I encountered a ton of difficulties. The issues were really diverse - from scheduling a learning time daily to effectively memorising the huge vocabulary lists. It was as challenging as it could get, even though I have a thing for learning new languages.

So, what did I do?

I researched and spent some time trying to work out a learning plan and came across several amazing strategies that looked promising indeed.

These brilliant techniques were simple, practical and, the best part was many of these could be practiced ON THE GO! Now, that was something which could fit in with a busy professional's hectic schedule.

Additionally, these tricks were quite interesting and easy to use.

And, guess what happened a few weeks down the lane?

I was getting BETTER and BETTER at my new language thanks to these tips and tricks. Still better, I can now communicate quite fluently and confidently in a language that I was quite apprehensive of, at first.

Over the past couple of years, I've even started teaching the language to scores of students along with these tips that helped me master it. Needless to say, these strategies have TREMENDOUSLY helped my students grasp and improve upon their targeted language skills.

Sounds great! Doesn't it?

It struck me then that these techniques could be powerful tools for anyone seeking to learn a new language and improve their communication skills.

In this ebook, there are 38 AWESOME and PROVEN strategies to help you on your language learning journey. A few of them may already seem familiar, but combine these with one or more of the others compiled below, and you are sure to see a REMARKABLE difference in your language skills!

So, READY, STEADY & GO!

Do you count yourself among those having one or more of the following difficulties when trying to communicate with others?

1.Difficulty in recalling the right vocabulary at the correct time and place. And, therefore, an associated degree of confusion, anxiety and nervousness when communicating.

2. Distinguish between different word usages (written vs oral)

3. Sentence formation with the correct tense of verbs

4. Translating to and fro the native language

5. Difficulty memorising huge word lists/synonyms, etc

Above all, how many times do we hold ourselves back from expressing our thoughts/ideas due to fear of using the wrong word/s?

Or, simply because you are quite unsure how and where to use your newly learnt vocabulary?

Well, first of all, know that you're not alone!

Your problem is something that scores of language learners face. The only difference is that with *time, consistent practice and use of the right techniques,* your language skills improve proportionally.

So, what's stopping you from investing in some daily time and practice towards language learning?

If you're ready to do so, I will share some of the most simple yet proven techniques that will help you improve your communication skills much beyond what you ever imagined!

Of course, there's no time-line guarantee involved.

But, one thing is for certain - If you follow the following tips and tricks, you are bound to improve on the issues that stop you from communicating fluently and with confidence.

So, are we ready?

I'm sure we are!

But before we delve in, here's what to EXPECT from this eBook:

1. *How to have better memory recall.*
2. *Boost your vocabulary list with advanced strategies.*
3. *Improved confidence and communication skills*
4. *Become a better speaker fast.*
5. *How to overcome the MOST common language learning issues.*
6. *Advanced techniques to help you improve your language skills all by yourself.*

38 Brilliant Techniques to Supercharge your Language & Communication Skills

1. The RLW (Read-Listen-Write) Technique:

READ -

First things first!

If you are someone who loves reading, then this should be a cakewalk for you.

Don't worry even if you are not!

So, for those who are fond of reading something or the other - be sure to expand on what you read. For eg: *journals, essays, articles,* etc. Not only will you be able to draw inspiration from the wonderful writing style that is observed in these journals, but also you can add many more words to your vocabulary list.

Additionally, subscribe to a good language learning blog and try to learn from its writing style and use of words.

But, go slow! (*Slow and steady wins the race!*)

More importantly, stick to stuff that you find interesting.

Also, try to have a daily reading routine of at least 30mins. (*Practice makes you perfect*)

Over time, you will notice your word power has progressed considerably. Besides, you are less likely to fumble in your vocabulary usage than before.

Another tip here is to try to learn the new and difficult words contextually. This way, you know when and how to use them better.

One good technique here is to note the new word down and revise it periodically.

When you read with greater awareness of the context, you tend to become better at identifying and organizing your communication skills effectively.

Needless to say, <u>Reading</u> is one of the most powerful techniques to improve your vocabulary long-term, literally by leaps and bounds!

For starters, try reading *"**Word Power Made Easy**"* by Norman Lewis. You can learn more about word formation and other vocabulary building aspects in a very interesting manner through this book.

Or *"**All About Words"*** by Maxwell Nurnberg and Morris Rosenblum is another good choice for . enriching your vocabulary by triggering your curiosity to build to your word list. There's also Barron's *"**GRE**"* which offers highly standardized vocabulary building techniques, one such being the use of flashcards. If reviews are anything to go by, then many have benefited in terms of their word power by using the flashcard technique.

The important thing to note here is to understand that building your vocabulary is an ongoing process and you need to be really passionate about it. So, each time you learn a new word, make at least 3-4 sentences around it so that you can remember it long-term.

LISTEN -

"Listening is a master skill for personal and professional greatness." -Robin Sharma

The virtues of listening as an important communication tool are immense.

Just imagine the confusion that would arise in effective communication when you haven't heard the speaker properly.

So, pay attention when someone speaks. This ensures the message is <u>clearly understood</u> for you to respond effectively. <u>Asking questions to clarify and using appropriate body language</u> when listening impacts the quality of your response to a large extent.

<u>Listening to podcasts, audiobooks, music</u>, etc is a great way to start thinking in English.
Doing this, you can really learn and improve your word list along with the right intonation and pronunciation.

Watching a TV series, educational videos/short films on YouTube, or even The News for building your vocabulary is also a good practice to know what's trending. However, try doing so along with subtitles until you don't really need them any longer.

In order to make this strategy more effective, watch TV or educational videos along with subtitles (at least in the beginning). Also, be sure to review and practice with your notes regularly.

WRITE -

<u>Writing daily</u> on a wide variety of interesting topics is something you should do if you are keen on building your written skills especially. You can also start off with writing a simple story about your routine and as you progress, pick some advanced topics.

"Reading maketh a full man; conference a ready man; and writing an exact man"

Of course, writing is a powerful way to <u>internalize your language learning.</u> Additionally, this is one strategy to <u>improve your English all by yourself</u>, without the need of a partner.

Practice your writing skills consistently and with feedback.

But how do you structure your article?

How do you keep the flow between your words?

And, more importantly, how do you engage your audience?

Start with the **why**: In other words, ask yourself *"what is my objective/goal in writing this article?"*

Your goal might be to inspire others, to share your experiences or a story or simply, you love writing!

No matter what your objective behind your writing might be, have clarity about the final purpose and why you are investing your time and energy into it.

More importantly, focus on writing *quality* content. The simple rule here being that your content trumps over your narrative skills or your flawless vocabulary.

What use is a beautifully worded article if it has actually no value for the audience?

So, when you create something valuable, loyalty and trust is built.

Also, try making your content more *relatable* to the audience. When your narrative is engaging and connects to not one but several end users, it becomes wonderfully compelling and attractive. Let your *authenticity* reflect in your writing, be it in terms of your *vocabulary choice* or flow of the narrative. Eventually, if you are just copying other content or writing something just for the heck of it, it does reflect in your writing.

So, let your honesty and logic reflect in your writing as they can connect to your audience much more long-term.

Focus on using the *right vocabulary* in what you write. A single word (*among vs between or assure vs ensure,* etc) can leave anyone confused.

Keep it short and simple, unless you want to really cramp up your article with a thousand ideas intertwined with redundant vocabulary.

Read and re-read to avoid any repetition or grammar mistakes. You can always work with a mentor who will give constructive feedback pertaining to your writing.

Not to forget using 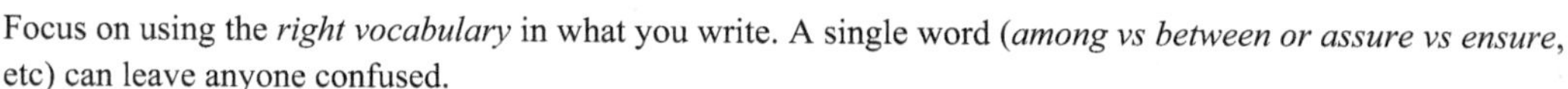 color codes in order to differentiate between words and remember them long-term.

Besides, remember to keep a dictionary handy to help you with new and difficult words.

And, more importantly, learn a word in all its tense forms and note it down in a journal, which you can review and practice with regularly.

For eg: Make sentences, write short essays or speak on a simple topic using these new words.

Writing not only builds your confidence in speaking English but also helps you gain fluency in speaking it.

So, you will slowly avoid using the redundant filler words and become a more effective speaker.

2.*Use 'New' words:*

Be sure to learn at least one word daily. Better still, learn five!

Wondering what next once you do that?

Practice using your new words in your daily conversations.

For eg: *I went for a stroll this morning.*

So here, you understand that the word *'stroll'* is a short *'walk'* that you generally take in the morning.

The children commute to their school by bus daily.

Commute is another word for *travel.*

By following this strategy, not only are you expanding your vocabulary list, but also at times when you forget a certain word, you know which one to use alternatively.

Review and practice your new word list either all by yourself or with a partner (preferably someone with good language skills). To do so, you can hide the definition of that word and check if you remember them, from time to time.

Or, you can ask your partner to ask you random words and see if you can remember their meanings. Practice with feedback will be a great help in the long run.

3.Make the Dictionary your Friend:

You can choose from a good and reliable dictionary online or offline. This is a great way to find multiple synonyms and antonyms for each new word. So, you can improve your word list and also learn where to use them.

For eg: You came across the word *'magnificent'* in your book.

Now, instead of this word, you can use *'splendid'*, *'wonderful'* or *'admirable'*.

Voila! You've learnt three additional words at a go!

So then, you can play around with the different meanings and usages of the new word.

For instance, observe these two sentences:

1. *I love her new shade of compact.*

2. *My new mobile is compact and trendy.*

In sentence 1. *'Compact'* is a *make-up accessory* and in sentence 2. The same word *'compact'* means *'sleek'*.

So again, learn the new words in context and practice using them along with their different meanings. This way, you can learn a word in all its different forms and usages.

Of course, English is sometimes a confusing language as a single word may have multiple synonyms that might make it all the more complicated. But, with a little practice daily, you will get better with time.

Also, if you have not already observed this fact about the English language, you may now notice that there are many synonyms to a specific word and they all look alike. Each word has its own unique usage. So, try to learn the little difference among those words to properly use that word in a given context without compromising its sense.

4. Niche Jargon:

When you learn a new word in context, you actually understand what its niche jargon stands for.

Take for example, words such as *'check-out'* which has different meanings in different scenarios (*Hotel, airport*, etc)

So, the next time you learn a new word, do so by understanding its context. This avoids the confusion that comes with a single word having multiple meanings in different scenarios.

For instance: *He weighs 140 pounds.*

The growing unemployment issue was weighing in on him.

Notice in the above sentences how the same word 'weight' can have different meanings. In the first statement, it means 'weight' and in the subsequent sentence it means 'troubling.'

This is where this strategy of learning words in context comes handy.

Eg: ***Railway station enquiry***:

-How much is the fare to X (destination)?

-What time is the train leaving?

Again, try using the new words as much as possible in your daily life communication.

For example, when ordering food at a restaurant, you can use specific jargon such as

'What's on the menu today?

Or

'Do you accept card or cash as payment mode?"

Also, start by saying the new word aloud, then relate it to a word you already know.

A good example of this is the word *gargantuan*, which means "*very large*" or "*gigantic*." Say a sequence aloud: *small, medium, large, very large, gargantuan.* Then list things you think are *gargantuan.*

Repeating a word aloud while reading it is a great practice to help it sink into your word list and become part of your daily conversations. Another benefit of this practice is that it adds to your confidence in speaking fluently.

5. **Learning Words through Play:**

Many board games such as *Scrabble, Last man standing, Word Bingo*, etc or apps such as *PowerVocab, Vocabulary.com* can help in learning a new language quite wonderfully.

There are many interesting games, quizzes, worksheets, and activities online which can help you widen your vocabulary knowledge.

My favorite among them is an activity involving the student to choose a new word and interpret it according to their understanding of the context.

For eg: if the student says 'I have *tremendous* respect for you.' Here, *tremendous* means *a lot of*.

And if the sentence is "a *tremendous* windstorm passed this town a few years back." Here, *tremendous* means *huge*.

So, as we have already learned above, the same word can mean differently in separate contexts. This technique is especially useful if you want to enhance your word list and get better with your communication in an interesting way.

6. **Flashcards**:

What do you do if you have to memorize a huge vocabulary list?

Well, a good idea would be to make the use of the conventional flashcards. Apart from being quite easy to make, flashcards can help you remember words or phrases contextually.

So by applying this strategy, you become more confident in handling real-life communication in English as the use of flashcards helps with random word usage.

And still better, if you don't want to create them yourself, there are plenty of online resources (apps, games, etc) that can make your life easier.

And, to help you use your flashcards effectively, there are plenty of proven techniques that can go a long way on your language learning journey.

7. **Online Courses**:

Look up online and you will find a plethora of online English courses that can be a great way to make your language learning objective much easier.

And wait, there are more benefits when you sign up for online English learning courses - You can learn staying where you are and at your own sweet pace. Besides, these online courses are very cost-efficient (as compared to classroom learning) and also quite engaging!

So, what are you waiting for?

Sign up for a reliable English learning course and see how it makes your communication hassle-free.

Additionally, you can find many English learning websites that can teach you the language in a highly interactive manner - for instance, through games, puzzles and fun quizzes.

Separately, practice speaking English with a language buddy online.

The best part of conversing with a language buddy is you have more often than not similar areas of interest. Additionally, you can give each other constructive and honest feedback about your language progress. This technique will not only make you more confident of your language skills fast but also learn the nuances of real-life spoken English.

8. **Make Use of Language Learning Apps**:

If you are someone who gets easily bored with classroom or other conventional forms of improving your language skills, then you can try out using language learning apps.

Choose your learning level - beginner, intermediate or advanced.

And, lo and behold!

You will find that there are diverse exercises and information available online suited to your level and learning objective.

And, don't worry! Your dependency on these apps will gradually decrease as you become increasingly fluent and confident in your communication skills over time. The best part is you can choose one or more apps according to your schedule, learning objective and requirement.

So, without much ado, let's delve into listing out the 10 best apps for helping you improve your English Language skills.

Best Apps for English Language Learning:

1. **Duolingo**: With over 85 million users learning English on this app, Duolingo has become the go-to app for language learning. Especially, via its gamification feature, you can learn new phrases, vocabulary, and sentences through games, earn points and move up the ranks. Another added benefit of this app is you can get to interact with other people with similar language learning goals.

2. **Busuu**: Here's another interactive language app that can help you learn a language on the go. You can practice your language skills loudly and repetitively using its speech recognition functionality. Other handy features that you can make use of here are digital flashcards and useful listening exercises.

3. **Babbel**: Learn English while having fun! Yes, you can learn English grammar, vocabulary, conversation dialogues using a single interface available either through their app or desktop. You can set the pace of your learning and make good use of their user-friendly video-based lessons and speech recognition tools.

4. **Grammarly**: If you have never heard of it, it's a powerful online grammar and spelling tool, to help you hone especially your writing skills. So, this can be a great app mainly for beginners in language learning. It's very easy to use and the best part is you get to know the exact reason behind even your tiniest grammar mistakes! Damn useful, I say!

5. **HelloEnglish**: Learn and improve your reading, writing and listening skills in English using the many audio and video exercises of this app. Plus, test your accent using the voice recognition tool. And, you can also listen to the language coming from the native speakers. Then, there are challenges or practice games in English, book reading exercises and dialogues for daily use.

6. **Memrise**: You can learn new vocabulary and phrases using this interactive app, and especially useful to help with improving your conversational skills. And, there's more. You will find language learning through flashcards highly engaging.

7. **Hello Talk**: Need a language buddy to practice your English language skills, then look no further. This app can help you get in touch with native speakers via chats or voice messages. So, a mobile phone is all you need to get started working on your communication skills in English.

8. **Learn English Vocabulary**: If you are a beginner looking to build your powerful vocabulary list in English, then this is an app you should be using. You won't find just extensive vocabulary to learn here. There are specialized modules to help you get better with your reading, writing, and speaking skills in English. You can learn English through flashcards which serve well for long-term memorization also.

9. **BBC Learning English**: Now, here's an app that helps with goal-oriented language learning. There are special modules for business English, Everyday English, and so on. You can keep yourself updated with the latest in vocabulary or sentence constructions. And then, there are also easy to understand transcripts and other tools to improve your vocabulary and pronunciation in English.

10. **iTalki**: Again, this is a highly flexible platform for practicing conversation online with native speakers of the English language. The best part is you can chat or Skype with your language buddy or take valuable English courses from professional teachers.

Conclusion:

There are multiple apps available online for free or paid, which can be really great for helping you with your language learning skills. And, as you progress you may really need them less and less. But, overall with the wide range of modules and tools available, these apps can be really useful in your language learning journey.

9. **Practice, Practice, Practice**:

What use is a language when you can't really speak it with someone?

Right?

So, if you are looking to immerse into a language and become great at it right from the basics, then start speaking it everywhere you find it feasible!

Honestly speaking, you have to forget about the fear of criticism or that of floundering while speaking. That's the commitment you need to be sure about while on your language learning journey.

A great practice here is to label everything possible around you, and try to recollect their names without referring to your labels. When you do this, you will slowly observe that you no longer struggle to remember a particular word and it all comes naturally to you.

Additionally, try practicing your language skills in your routine conversations as much as you can. This way, you will become a more confident speaker quickly.

You can also combine this technique with several other proven techniques to practice and improve your English all by yourself!

More importantly, don't be afraid of making mistakes or be too conscious of grammar and vocabulary errors when you speak. Remember that with every mistake you make, you only progress towards your learning goal.

And if it helps, make this popular adage your success mantra, *"Rome wasn't built in a day!"*

10. **Learn with Synonyms & Spellings**:

Another great way to improve your word power is to learn a new word along with its synonyms and spellings in different accents. So, most commonly the words that end with an unstressed *-our* in British English end with *-or* in American English.

For example: The words 'odor' and 'humor' in American English are 'odour' and 'humour' in British English.

Understanding this difference in spelling of the same word in different accents can really prevent a lot of confusion when using them.

And, of course, knowing the different synonyms of a single word when learning it can have its own advantages. You have a wider and more sophisticated choice of word usage in your communication.

Needless to say, using this strategy can really help you build your vocabulary fast and effectively.

11. **Mind Maps:**

Mind mapping is an interesting technique that can help you become a more effective English learner. In fact, this unique strategy makes the language learning process more simpler and more natural. Here's how to use it in making your language sound more polished and impressive:

Mind mapping is a powerful language learning tool that comprises of simple graphical representations that help understand any specific topic in a much better manner easily. Information is organized such that it shows a clear association between ideas, words, and concepts.

Attractive and bright visual diagrams are drawn around a core idea/thought which helps you remember things long-term. For eg: popular software tools such as Roam Research organizes your information more productively. No wonder then, this tool can be used for language learning effectively too.

Without a doubt, these thinking maps are great tools to help you build on your word list. Let's see how:

As mind maps create more organised data, it becomes easier to manage your huge vocabulary lists. It just mimics how you remember vocabulary in your native language - through connections, not through lists, meaning it feels more natural, works more effectively, and is also more interesting to use.

Let's say, you wanted to find the various synonyms for the word "*talk*".

Under the topic of '*talk*', you can add related categories such as "*keep quiet*", "*public lecture*", etc.

Further connected keywords and phrases such as "*lecturing*", "*spill the beans*", and so on could be joined with this network, so that you create a map of related words and phrases.

Mind-mapping means that it's easier to remember different, related words, through remembering the connections between them.

Traditional '*vocabulary learning*' involves long lists of unrelated words, with their meaning. No wonder people find it so difficult and boring to try to memorise and remember each one.

However, using mind maps, you can enjoy the process of visualising and creating an entire list of related words, in a very effective manner.

You can even go one step further, and create mind maps for different topics, such as *'food'*, *'clothing'*, *'colours'*, and so on.

Each such topic will have its own related definitions, sample sentences, spellings, notes and useful links.

Depending upon how far you are interested to explore, mind maps can have multiple subcategories which can be updated regularly as you come across new words.

For example, under the term *"clothing"*, you can have familiar subcategories such as *"clothes for summer"*, *"clothes for winter"*, *"clothes for the rainy season"*, etc.

Further under the subcategory *"clothes for summer"*, you can add related words such as *"clothes for the beach"*, *"holiday clothes"* and so on.

Remember those fun books you used to have as a kid, with the words for each object there for you to learn? It works because you learn related words in context - mind mapping works on a very similar principle.

12. **Learn a New Word with All its Tenses:**

When should you use '*have, had or has*'?

Or, what's the difference between say, '*parked*' and '*had parked*'?

If you are someone who has a hard time remembering the verb tenses at the appropriate time, then you should try the following technique:

Every time you come across a new word, try learning it along with its *present, past and future tenses*. Try to remember the names of tenses as you learn them. Note down regular and irregular verbs in the first person singular form for all the tenses (i.e., I).

Then, write an article/essay/story/letter, etc using the different/at least one tense form. Try to play around with question words, helping verbs (*have, has, had*) and sentences beginning with '*if.*"

Applying this technique, you will find that you are getting better with your sentence constructions. No longer are you confused which tense goes best with a particular scenario. And above all, there's more clarity and sharpness in your communication as you will be better able to put forward your ideas/thoughts.

13.Remove Filler Words:

Most of the time, consciously or not, we tend to use redundant words such as *'basically', 'like', 'okay', 'right',* etc. These crutch or filler words are meant to fill those avoidable silences in your speech. In fact, there is a complete list of authorized filler words which you can go ahead and use in your communication.

However, filler words become a problem when they are used as a cover for nervousness or lack of clarity.

It tends to get distracting for the listener when you use a lot of *"like', "you know'* etc.

Isn't it?

In fact, it severely handicaps your effective communication skills.

The simple rule to speaking good English (or for that matter, any language) is to avoid using filler words in our speech.

A good way to start doing this is to prefer having a pause in your speech over using these filler words. During this pause, you can collect your thoughts, gather your nerves and also give your audience a brief moment to sink into your ideas.

Another great way is to record yourself speaking and play it so that you become more aware of those unnecessary words in your speech. The more you become conscious of these words, the greater care you will take in order to avoid them the next time around.

You can also practice your speech beforehand with pauses instead of the filler words and note the difference it makes to your overall communication.

Yet another simple way to eliminate a crutch word (for eg: *very*) is to consciously stop using it and pave the way to learn alternative new words instead.

For eg:

Instead of *she's very tired,* use "she is exhausted."

Don't say *"The injury was very painful"*. Instead try saying "The injury was excruciating."

In the above examples, not only have you eliminated a filler word *"very"*, but also learnt new words to replace it.

This technique makes you sound more impressive and confident by avoiding the unnecessary words in your communications and gives you more control over the conversation.

14. **Patterned Repetition**:

Repetition is the key.

Research says that on an average, it takes between 10 and 20 repetitions for a new word to become a part of your memory. However, in today's world, we prefer fast-paced and handy methods for anything, including language learning.

So, here comes the ***spaced repetition software***, which has similar functionality such as the traditional *flashcards system*, but is more advanced and manageable. Using this learning technique, you can revise something at regular intervals. *AnkiDroid, Quizlet, Memorion*, etc - there are multiple tools that are available online that offer the SRS feature. The software runs on the principle that repeated exposure to something leads to a more long-term memory recall of it.

The best part is that you don't need to be really tech-savvy to leverage this tool. Anyone keen to learn a language on the go can use this tool effectively.

Alternately, writing the new word down along with its meaning and sample sentence can help it sink into your memory more long-term. You can start practicing this technique in your daily written or verbal communication (emails, routine conversations, etc)

15. **Use connectors**:

Connectors in your speech such as *moreover, additionally, overall, in conclusion*, etc. can help further streamline your thought process very effectively.

Using these linking words, you can emphasize a key point, direct the flow of your speech, present your viewpoint or conclusion, and make your speech sound more engaging.

There are many types of language connectors such as:

CAUSE & EFFECT

For: Rob came drenched *for* it was raining heavily that morning.

Because: The woman loves gardening *because* she finds it liberating.

As: The boy didn't turn up for school *as* he was unwell.

Since: He didn't get the job *since* he didn't have the necessary educational qualifications for it.

Therefore: She submitted her homework on time. *Therefore*, she wasn't reprimanded by the teacher.

Hence: This class is very diligent. *Hence*, everyone likes it.

As a result: It was pouring heavily today morning. *As a result*, the turnout at the exhibition was poor.

Consequently: They had fought yesterday. *Consequently*, they aren't on talking terms currently.

Due to: She couldn't repay her loan on time *due to* her financial constraints.

Because of: This particular celebrity is often the object of attention *because of* his peculiar attitude.

As a result of: *As a result of* poor sales, the show was canceled soon.

So: He dozed off while listening to the story, *so* he didn't know its ending.

Thus: The pandemic scared the townsfolk. ***Thus***, there was a mass exodus.

CONTRAST

But: She was beautiful ***but*** behaved strangely.

Although: Although it was located in a remote place, the house was beautiful.

Despite: They were a happy family ***despite*** the fact that they were damn poor.

However: He had worked hard for the job. ***However***, he couldn't get through the interview.

Nevertheless: The poor exam results were demotivating. ***Nevertheless***, he kept working harder.

Yet: He had the best facilities any child could get, ***yet*** he could never really make it big in life.

Apart from: ***Apart from*** being one of the richest in town, he was known to be quite humble too.

Whereas: All the houses in that area were huge, whereas his house was small but cozy.

Alternatively: You can make an appointment online. *Alternatively*, you can call him up directly.

On the contrary: It was a well-developed town. *On the contrary*, it's people were quite orthodox, sometimes radical-minded too.

ILLUSTRATION

In this case: *In this case,* no discrepancy was ever observed.

Such as: There are different types of connectors *such as*...

As an example: *As an example* of his saying, he cited an old folktale.

Illustrated by: The population growth over the years can well be *illustrated by* this chart.

For instance: The city's pollution had increased considerably. *For instance*, a thick pall of smoke can be seen everywhere nowadays.

In the case of : The impact of global warming can already be seen, *as in the case* of major environmental changes happening in the world.

For example: Almost every country is slowly inching towards improving literacy levels. *For example...*

ADDITION

As well as: He was dashingly handsome *as well as* extremely rich.

And: The forest is thick *and* beautiful.

Too: It was humid and raining *too*.

In addition to: The woman got a lot of other benefits *in addition to* monetary compensation.

Furthermore: It has rained heavily this time. *Furthermore*, there have been floods in some areas too.

Also: He was qualified and deserving. *Also*, he had worked hard for this job.

Not only-But also: The boy was *not only* naughty *but also* a habitual liar.
Or: You can have either tea *or* coffee.

EMPHASIS

More importantly: The government took serious steps in terms of the pandemic. *More importantly*, the public was made aware of the gravity of the situation.

Notably: He was very good with accounts. **Notably**, he hardly made any errors in his ledgers.

In particular: There was a public outcry against the government. **In particular**, people were upset with the bureaucratic procedures.

Significantly: We've come a long way in terms of literacy levels over the years. *Significantly*, this has impacted our standards of living too.

Indeed: He had struggled hard for it. *Indeed*, it was a great achievement on his part.

Especially: We need to take precautions on hygiene issues, *especially* now.

Above all: His humility and generosity floored everyone. *Above all*, it was his compassion that struck a chord with the audience.

OPINION

I think: *I think* we can make more efforts for rehabilitation of the needy.

I believe: *I believe* the liberalization policy has opened up many doors for most countries of the world.

I feel: *I feel* we should all come together in our fight against this crisis.

In my opinion: *In my opinion*, he's the best football coach we could afford to have.

It seems to me: *It seems to me* that he has genuinely put efforts in his work.

It seems likely that: *It seems likely that* there was a massive natural disaster that wiped the dinosaurs completely from the earth.

As far as I know: *As far as I know*, she's a very honest person.

COMPARISON

Likewise: Tom was good at his studies. *Likewise*, he was a good football player too.

Similarly: The old school was in bad shape in terms of several repair works needed. Similarly, it also needed an efficient teaching staff.

In the same way: Their children were diligent. In the same way, they were extremely responsible and bright.

Equally: She worked hard for her family. Equally, she put in extra efforts at her workplace too.

Like: The company was very considerate towards his health condition. *Like* it went out of its way to offer support to him and his family.

Despite this: The boy was hardly literate. *Despite this*, he had made it big in his life.

Of contrast: He was a talented musician. *Of contrast*, was his extreme stinginess.

Contrarily: The judge was unbiased in his judgement. *Contrarily*, he did offer a lenient parole to the convict.

PERSUASION

Of course: I've just made a marshmallow cake. *Of course*, you can have a bite!

Certainly: He's really well-settled in his life now. *Certainly*, he deserves this.

Undoubtedly: She won the beauty pageant hands down. *Undoubtedly*, she's a rare mix of beauty and brains.

Indeed: I've heard so much about the wonderful steak they make at the restaurant. *Indeed*, we must try it sometime soon.

Decidedly: She was both experienced and qualified. *Decidedly*, she opted to become a home-maker and take care of her family.

Surely: The children have really worked hard for their exams. *Surely*, they deserve this treat.

Evidently: He showed his dismal first term exam results to his parents. *Evidently*, they were disappointed big-time.

Clearly: She's worked on her culinary skills over the years. *Clearly*, she's no less than a master chef now!

SEQUENCE

Firstly: There are many glaring issues in the world currently. *Firstly*, unemployment is a major concern globally.

Then: It was just a barren piece of land. *Then*, people came and houses sprung up everywhere.

Next: To combat the climate change issue, we need to create more awareness. *Next*, we have to own up our individual responsibilities.

Afterwards: He came home tired from work that day. *Afterwards*, he went out to meet his friends.

Eventually: All our efforts towards protecting the environment today will *eventually* lead to better long-term prospects.

Previously: He started work in the software department. *Previously*, he was a mechanical engineer.

Finally: The organization had started small. *Finally*, it did rise up the ranks with good planning and operations.

16.Online Language Courses:

"Knowledge of languages is the doorway to wisdom." - Roger Bacon

Effective communication comes through a good grasp over the language along with a great idea or thought formulation. When you improve on your language skills, it reflects in the way you communicate - your body language, gestures and how effectively you are able to send across your message to the recipient.

Besides the techniques described in this ebook, a good way to brush up on your language skills is to sign up for a good and reliable online language course.

Look up online and you will find a plethora of online English courses that can be a great way to make your language learning objective much easier and engaging too. These are pocket friendly and can be taken from anywhere in the world with just a good Internet connection.

And, the results are amazing. From being a good platform to connect with other people having similar interests/goals to helping you overcome your inhibitions, online language courses are a great way to enhance your language and communication skills.

Also, you can find many English learning websites that can teach you the language in a highly interactive manner - for instance, through games, puzzles and fun quizzes.

Alternately, practice speaking English with a language buddy online. It will not only make you more confident of your language skills fast but also learn the nuances of real-life spoken English. This way you will not fumble in remembering a particular word at the right time or fill up your speech with redundant words.

17. Use Phrasal Verbs:

Phrasal verbs are different combinations of a verb, adverb, preposition and/or a noun. Examples of commonly used phrasal verbs are: *bring up, break down, carry on*, etc.

Why should you use them?

Well, there are multiple reasons for using phrasal verbs, especially because they are commonly used in informal communication and they make your sentences sound more impressive and natural.

But, they can end up being very confusing sometimes as they have multiple meanings in different contexts.

For eg: Her children had really *let her down* at the party. (meaning: disappointed her)

Joyce let *her guard down* at the ball yesterday evening. (carefree)

Further, phrasal verbs are different in meaning from the individual verbs which constitute them.

For eg: '*Look down'* is a phrasal verb which means consider someone unworthy whereas the verb '*look*' means to '*stare* or *glare*'.

List of Commonly Used Phrasal Verbs:

So, here we go,

1. **Count on** = Depend on

Eg: You can *count on* me whenever you need something.

2. **Ask out** = invite someone to go out with you (eg: for a dinner, movie, etc).

Eg: He *asked her out* for a movie that evening.

3. **Bring on**: To cause something to happen.

Eg: He alleged she was *bringing on* disrepute to the family.

4. **Put off**: Evade replying to something/unpleasant experience.

Eg: Anna was *put off* by Harry's unusual behavior that day.

Or,

Her father *put off* responding to her queries for as long as possible.

5. **Call off:** Cancel

Eg: Unfortunately, their wedding was *called off* unceremoniously.

6. **Back up**: Support; Stand by

Eg: The mayor was *backed up* by his team at a time of crisis.

Or,

Do you have an inverter *back up*, just in case?

7. **Blow up**: Fill up something; Blast

Eg: The scandal soon got *blown up out* of proportions.

8. **Hang up**: Close; Block

Eg: He abruptly *hung up* her call, when she spoke bitterly.

9. **Put away**: Confine; Divert

Eg: He quickly *put away* the negative thoughts.

10. **Fill in**: Reply in writing

Eg: He had to *fill in* all his details in the questionnaire at the customs office.

11. **Agree with**: Concur; Approve

Eg: Surprisingly, the football team *agreed with* all the new rules laid down.

12. **Bail out**: Help; Release

Eg: His lawyer *bailed him out* the same evening when he was jailed.

13. **Opt in**: Choose

Eg: Jane *opted in* to take care of all the work in the manager's absence.

14. **Come across**: Encounter; Find

Eg: There was a very unusual man that he *came across* that morning.

15. **Drop by**: Visit

Eg: Her aunt *dropped by* her house for lunch.

16. **Catch up**: Meet; Approach

Eg: The group of friends *caught up* with each other after a long time.

17. **Add up to**: Sum up; Amount to

Eg: All his hard work *added up to* nothing in the end!

18. **Carry on**: Continue an activity

Eg: Despite the heavy rains, they *carried on* with the building construction activity.

19. **Get along with**: Be in harmony; Agree

Eg: They both *got along with* each other as a house on fire.

20. Breakthrough: Achieve success in something.

Eg: The police team achieved a major *breakthrough* in the murder case.

18. **Immersion**:

Learning anything becomes an interesting process when it seems effortless and engaging.

Right?

So, surround yourself in a language learning atmosphere. This way, it becomes a habit to speak, write, read, and listen to only English for a specified duration each day consistently.

And, you don't have to visit or stay at foreign shores to learn the native language naturally.

You can do so staying right where you are (while having fun)!

And, how?

Through the highly popular Language Immersion Techniques!

Conventionally, in the 1960s, people in Canada preferred their children to learn a language through understanding/knowing it in totality. In other words, rather than focussing on the language itself, the objective was towards holistic communication.

Knowing a culture is still a great way to delve further into learning a new language effectively with greater impetus on integrating the core of language learning rather than superficiality. Language immersion became relative to living in the country of the targeted language, getting to know better of its culture and traditions and thereby, allowing the language to sink organically.

But, do you really need to move to foreign shores to learn a language?

And, what if you are still finding it difficult to learn the language?

Fret not at all!

Keep your worries and inhibitions aside! You can learn a new language staying where you are with the different Language Immersion techniques! Consistent practice of these proven strategies go a long way in helping you learn the targeted language in a much more interesting and fun way!

So, what is Language Immersion?

It simply means learning a new/foreign language in its totality. A very popular bilingual mode of giving instructions, language immersion has been known to break new ground in the individual's decision making abilities, besides fortifying their command over the language. The ultimate objective of language immersion is to make the communication in that language very interactive and natural, speaking the language proficiently and gaining a thorough knowledge of the culture and traditions of the targeted language.

So, isn't the idea of moving to foreign shores to sink into the local surroundings in order to learn its language a little too demanding?

And, totally in agreement with the above idea, here's a list of the top language immersion strategies, which you can start with right NOW and without having to go anywhere!

Top Language Immersion Techniques -

1. **Delve into it** - Yes, you heard that right! Forget about learning a language through focus on its grammar and vocabulary only. Rather, ensuring that the overall surroundings are conducive to learning. There are many ways to do this. For instance, by changing the language settings on your phone, computer or any electronic gadget (including video games!) to the targeted language will work wonders for starters. By doing this, you can explore and learn the unique vocabulary and usage in an interesting way. But, do remember to keep your dictionary handy, but not depend too much on it.

Another great idea would be to watch your favourite movies/TV shows or just about anything along with the subtitles.

Or, if you are a reading buff, try including books, online journals or magazines in your targeted language.

Also, you could write your daily journal (if you already do), grocery lists, and so on in the language you want to learn.

And yes, hone your listening skills is another great language immersion technique which you can do along with your regular work. Podcasts, audiobooks, music...the list is endless, when it comes to learning a new language through listening!

2. **Consistent Practice**: The ease and interest factor in language immersion comes through consistently practicing it with someone, (preferably who's already good at it). Again, if you don't have a speaking partner, you could do a role-play all by yourself on topics such as culture, cuisine, etc. Better still, you could sing songs or narrate stories, all in the targeted language. But, no matter what you do, remember not to worry about making mistakes or whether you are doing it right! Remember, you learnt your familiar language in a similar fashion, making a ton of mistakes and reworking on them until you got it right. (Right?)

3. **Go local with apps**: You can always take the help of immensely useful apps such as Bilingua, where you could practice your language skills with a native speaker. The best part is that there is a scope for having interesting conversations around a common area of interest. Or, you could sign up for online toastmasters or maybe speaking clubs of your targeted language. Facebook groups are another great option to meet other like-minded people seeking to learn a language, besides having a hearty discussion on common areas of interests.

4. **Sign up for a language immersion program**: There are scores of language immersion programs that you can find online. By joining such programs, you can not not access their community of similar people seeking language learning, but learn about the latest trends and tips that go a long way helping you on your language learning journey.

5. **Mind reprogramming:** Last, but certainly not the least, programming your mindset so that you think in the targeted language is definitely something you should take seriously if you want to learn a new language quickly. For instance, if English is a language you are looking to learn, then you need to start practicing the language a part of your routine.

In a Cosmopolitan world, language immersion comes as a remarkably powerful tool to learn a language in its entirety, giving due weightage to its culture and background.

As Goethe said, *"He who knows no foreign language knows nothing of his own."*

19.**Find a Language Buddy**:

"Learning a new language is becoming a member of the club – the community of speakers of that language."

– Frank Smith

Do you often wish you had someone with whom you could practice your language skills without any fear of being ridiculed?

Yes, language learning becomes more interesting and fun if you can practice it with someone who has similar learning goals or objectives as you.

So then, find a good language buddy online for practice. It's fun to discuss diverse topics, debate, or just engage in a mock quiz to make it more engaging.

Also, Toastmasters online is another great platform where you can practice your language skills with other people. You can get a good command over the language with practice and also hone your communication skills through impromptu conversations and speeches.

That's not all!

There's never a dearth of several engaging activities attuned towards your personality development goals and helping you grow your social network.

Another great idea is to find someone from your acquaintances who's already good at the language and practice having conversations in English with them. Remember to take feedback on your progress from time to time.

This strategy can really take your goal (whether it is language learning or communication skills improvement) to a level with more clarity and precision.

20. **Set Goals for your Learning**:

As with anything else you want to achieve, a goal-oriented language learning reaps rich benefits.

Start with simple. Maybe learn one new word each day or try to speak at least 5 sentences in your targeted language to begin with.

Then, as you progress, you can improvise on your learning objectives. For instance, specify a time period for your learning curve or get to a certain level of vocabulary by a certain time line.

Whether your learning objective is to improve your writing skills or overall communication, your goal needs to be realistic and result-oriented. Also, a little flexibility never harms.

Most importantly, it should fit in with your schedule and learning requirement, so that you enjoy the whole process of learning and improvising upon the desired skill/s.

21.Record yourself Speaking in English and Review Regularly:

Well, this is a great way to learn a language, especially if you don't have a speaking partner.

All you have to do is practice speaking on a topic for a specified duration, as frequently as you can.

Different tremendously powerful strategies can help you ramp up on your language skills. A few of them are:

Mirroring:

Stand before a mirror and imagine you have just walked into a doctor's clinic. How would you start your conversation at the reception? What would be your responses at the doctor's questions? How would you describe your condition? Etc. Duplicating such scenarios, preparing on the communication, and repetition of role-plays on a regular basis goes a long way in improving your gait and tone of your speech!

JAM/Role-Play Techniques:

Did you know the Just-a-Minute (JAM) technique is a very powerful tool to improve your command over English, or for that matter, any language you want to learn?

- You speak on a topic (anything simple, or close to your heart, to begin with!) for a minute. You can set the timer so as to stick to the time limit.
- Then, write down a few pointers on the same topic. For example, if the topic chosen was 'Family', you can write down reference points such as : nuclear/joint family, caring, close-knit, etc.
- Record yourself this time around, speaking with the help of the above reference points.
- Do this multiple times in a day to improve your command and confidence over the language.

Role-Play:

Another equally, (if not more!) powerful strategy to improve your English language skills is enacting a character. It can be a role in your daily life which you frequently come across or something you wish to prepare yourself with more appropriate communication on. For example, booking tickets online, hotel reservations, at the doctor's clinic, Interview, shopping, etc - these are all situations in your daily life where you may need to converse in English and maybe finding it difficult to do so! If you don't have a partner to practice your conversation with, you can do it by yourself too!

22. **Break Difficult Vocabulary into Parts**:

And yes, practice it until you get it right!

For eg: "*Hallucinations*" can be broken into "*hall-oo-cee-na-tions.*"

Then practice forming sentences with the difficult word such as:

"*She used to have hallucinations regularly.*"

You can really build a strong vocabulary list by breaking it down into simple syllables. But, remember, it is not always the case that the broken syllables of a word are meaningful or make sense.

For eg: *comprehensive - (com-pre-hen-siv); expansion - (ex-pan-sion), wednesday - (wens-day),* etc

Therefore, the only aim of this technique is to recall long words or spellings and know when a certain letter goes silent (as in *wednesday*, spelt as *wensday*).

23. **Read the Editor's Column**:

How many times have you brushed past the Editor's column of your favorite Daily without having a look at it?

If yes, then do you know that it is a great place for the latest in vocabulary or trending language practices?

Remember to note down a new or difficult word you come across and practice with it in your written or oral communication as much as possible. Another good strategy here is to read the entire column and write it in your own words. This way you can develop your reading comprehension and writing skills.

So, if you want to build upon your vocabulary, don't miss on the Editor's Column!

24. **Sing along with English Music**:

Do you lip-sync to music often?

Then, try it with some English songs. You can take the help of sub-titles/transcripts or take a printout of the lyrics while singing along. Just remember to choose songs that have simple words, easy to understand and in everyday English.

This strategy is especially useful if you are looking to improve your vocabulary in an interesting way. Not only do you come across new words when you listen to songs, but also get more clarity on their intonations and pronunciation!

And, if you are specifically working on improving a certain accent (british, american, etc), then choose your music accordingly.

25. **Replay your Day**:

Before you go to bed, every night you can replay the entire events of your day.

And, how do you do it?

By thinking and making your statements in English!

For eg: "*I had a busy day today*", "*I woke up early today*", etc.

Try to relate and connect with how you are feeling.

For eg: *Granny was excited to see us at her house.*

How can you say the same statement in a different, possibly better way?

Maybe something like this:

"*Granny was delighted/thrilled at seeing us at her house.*"

There, your vocabulary list is richer by two other words (*delighted, thrilled*)

And, that's exactly how you can have more vocabulary at hand in order to sound more fluent and impressive. Not just that, this technique can make you more of a natural speaker and help you communicate better in your daily life conversations.

26. The Expression Technique:

Our emotions and feelings that come out in the open as our expressions are indeed a good way to work with our language and communication skills.

How?

Take any regular day in your life and think of the diverse emotions you go through in it - happiness, excitement, sorrow, boredom, etc. If you could start verbalizing these emotions/expressions, imagine how easy it would be for more advanced communication skills.

For instance, You've just witnessed your mom getting really angry at something.

This can be stated as *"Mom pursed her lips and clenched her fists tightly. And by the time I could realize what was going on, she had erupted like a fireball."*

Thus, your statement sounds so wonderful, with all the expressions right in place and exactly depicting someone's state of mind.

This strategy is really helpful to build a powerful vocabulary and also in daily life sentence formations.

In addition, observe the world around you and find the synonyms of the new words that you learn each day.

Observation of the self and others is a very powerful way to learn a language, in fact more reliable than reading. This might relate to someone's expression (happy, sad, upset, etc).

For eg: You just had the most delicious spaghetti some time ago. You can express it in any or more of the following ways:

"The spaghetti was simply awesome/delectable/heavenly"

However, this technique doesn't imply trying to skim through dictionaries for learning hard words.

Having fun while practicing your language skills is the best way you can really learn a language.

27. **Take Dictations**:

How do you assess your progress in terms of language or communication skills from time to time?

By taking down dictations periodically. In other words, you listen to some spoken input and write it down.

You can always take the help of a friend or search online for many such dictation tests. But remember to take down something really worth it. For instance, speeches, audiobooks, podcasts, etc.

Another good technique you can try here is to read aloud as you write. Also, once you are done writing your essay/speech, you can try to speak about it in your own words. Of course, you can refer to a certain good phrase or quote here or there, but try to build your own sentences as much as possible. This way, you are working with your natural speaking skills and fluency as well.

There's one more strategy you can use here. Read something in your familiar language and translate it in your own words in your targeted language. For this, you can also rephrase a stanza from your local daily (in your native language/mother tongue) taking the help of a dictionary (online or not).

Taking dictations is really a very powerful technique as you can improve on three different language and communication skills at one time - listening, writing and speaking skills!

Sounds wonderful? Then, try this simple technique now!

28. Recitation:

Are you an aspiring poet or writer? Or you are someone who loves talking? So, why not converse in English, rather than your familiar language?

Why not recite a poem or a story or just something in English? Recitation is when you read something aloud and/or repeat from your memory. However, remember that recitation is not simply reading. When reciting, you need to be really careful of your pitch, pace, intonation, pronunciation and rhythm of your speech. Here, you are speaking impromptu based on your understanding of the topic in your memory.

So, this is another well-known strategy to improve your English without a speaking partner! This technique not only is supposed to help you improve on your command over the language but also goes a long way in helping you think in English in a relaxed way!

And wait, it's not all.

It helps in better memory recall as it develops patterns and sequences of whatever you are reciting. Above all, it adds to your confidence and body language and makes you more of a natural speaker.

29. **Take Mock Tests Online**:

As you build on your language skills, you need to regularly assess your proficiency so that you know that you are right on track with your learning objective.

Online mock tests are a great way to do that! You can take them after completing every module or as frequently as you can. You get instant answer evaluations and feedback after every test, which is a good indicator of your proficiency level achieved.

There are other advantages of taking online tests too:

A. *Gives you an honest estimate of your concept understanding.*
B. *Convenience*
C. *Builds confidence*

This strategy is especially useful if you want to check how well you are progressing in terms of your learning objectives.

30.Learn at least One New Word Daily:

Or more!

And, with its synonyms (and antonyms, if possible)

Make it a goal to do this and you will see how tremendously your vocabulary has improved in a short time.

So, how do you go about this technique?

The simplest way is to Read! Yes, read upon different and interesting topics (online or not). Read something that you haven't so far, which helps you build unique vocabulary.

When you start adding new words to your database, you will be amazed at how fluent your communication has become! Try it!

31. **Root Words:**

Try to analyse the etymology or the core meaning of a word (the root) as you learn it. Root words are formed by adding prefixes or suffixes to a base word. Learning a single root or basic word can help you learn and understand multiple words consisting of this word. So, you can understand how richer your vocabulary will be when you learn around 30 or more root words.

For eg: In the word **'democracy'**, the greek origin of this word is **'dem'**, which means popular. So, this is the root word for '*democracy.*' Or, the word 'acting' consists of the root word '**act**' and suffix *-ing*. On similar lines, in the word '*transport*' - *port* (to carry) is the root word.

Knowing these root words will help you expand on your vocabulary base very quickly.

This technique is very useful when you want to improve your vocabulary quickly with a greater understanding of the language basics.

32. **Maintain a Journal**:

What do you do when you come across a new word? If you have already not done it, then do this now!

Note all your new words in a journal that you can refer to from time to time. Build simple to complex statements using this vocabulary as you progress towards your learning goals. In addition, you can note down useful idioms and contextual phrases for daily conversations.

For instance, you can note down helpful communication on real-life scenarios such as *"book a hotel room'*, *'at the railway station'*, *"airport communication'*, etc. Do practice upon these entries regularly so that when you are in some such context, you are more confident than ever.

Another good thing to write in your journals is about your daily life experiences, emotions, etc. Try playing around with simple to complex words and statements when you write. This serves as a great indicator of your progress when you refer to it much later on your learning curve.

Again, all these are really great ways to improve your memory recall. Besides, noting down your new words and learning regularly is an engaging experience for you as well.

33. **Label Everything**:

As someone learning a new language when you look around, you see a world of objects whose name you're not sure of. And, when you have to make use of one or more of these in your regular communication, it really becomes difficult.

Because either you don't seem to remember the name or you are racking your brains for a better word up instead.

So, this strategy is especially for those who are new to language learning. When you attach post-its or label anything around you, it becomes a good reference the next time you want to use it in your conversation. There are also many online tools for you to make use of.

Do this as frequently as possible on anything around you and see the huge difference it makes to your confidence while speaking.

Also, this is a wonderful way to build upon your vocabulary list naturally and add new and unique words to your memory.

34. **Join Toastmasters**:

Toastmasters online is a great platform if you are looking to improve your language skills and build your confidence when speaking publicly. There are a variety of resources here that not only support your learning goals but also help you gain a competitive edge at work.

These forums are great places to hone your communication skills via their highly useful podcasts, webinars and public speaking tips. Then, there are a lot of engaging activities such as speech contests that are a great indicator of your progress.

Of course, using this resource, you can get over your inner hesitation to speak up in public and build up your network and confidence levels too!

35. **Useful Resources:**

Without a doubt, Merriam-Webster, Vocabulary.com, Mnemonic Dictionary and Thesaurus.com are very popular for those looking for an online dictionary or a reference resource for looking up on an idiom or phrase.

You can download useful apps such as Magoosh vocabulary app or Barron's 1100 for GRE.

Additionally, the following websites can also be helpful companions on your language learning journey - Wordpandit, Memrise, Hitbullseye.com and Visuwords.com. Not only do these websites and apps have wonderful games and quizzes to help you learn English in a fun and interesting manner, but also are quite engaging too.

Another really fun way to learn English is to create a personal Whatsapp group where the only participant is YOU! Keep adding all your new vocabulary, cool jargons, idioms, question words, etc to this group as and when you come across them.

And Voila! You've just created a handy reference for all your language learnings.

36. Mnemonics:

What is Mnemonics?

A word or image association with something in your language learning helps you remember it better in the long-term. Isn't it? Mnemonics is exactly this concept of connecting a new word or sentence with an idea or pattern, thus enabling better recall factor.

How do you remember a word such as *"scurry"* (which means *to run in quick and short steps*)?

Associate it with easily visual or acoustic cues such as :

I **scurry** with my pet furry on our daily walk.

You can easily use Mnemonics to associate a linking word with an image so that you can remember it long-term. Mnemonics can help improve your vocabulary and pronunciation and also better memory retention.

37.Visualize New Words:

Another powerful technique to improve your word power is to create a mental picture of any new word or scenario that you come across. These visual cues will help you whenever you want to recall that word, besides being useful in reading comprehension and retention. You can also connect the new word with a drawing or even a vocabulary flash card.

Eg: For a word such as *'mountain'*, you can associate it with a visual image of climbing (prefix-"*mount*"), thus, whenever you come across this word, the associated linked image will help you remember it easily.

You can also visualize common conversation scenarios such as *'at the restaurant', 'airport lounge' or 'booking a hotel room.'* Or you can practice on topics such as *'describe someone', 'your hobbies'*, etc. Refer to a script or pointers before you relax and visualize the same.

At a physiological level, this strategy combines both of your right and left brain functions and makes the learning process more interesting. This is because when visualizing, you are more relaxed and receptive. So, you can enjoy the process and also have better memory recall.

This technique is especially useful for building confidence when speaking and helps you communicate more naturally.

38. Have Fun:

Without a doubt, this one is a must-have on your to-do list of language learning. When you enjoy the process of learning a language, there is less effort required. Besides, you are more receptive and able to grasp things easily.

Isn't it?

So, go ahead and learn English but don't forget to have fun too!

THANK YOU!

Thank you for reading this ebook - *'How to Improve your Language Skills & Speak Effectively!'*

In this ebook, I have shared my personal learnings and experiences as an English Language trainer for more than 5 years. And, I hope that this book has contributed towards improving your communication skills and helped you in your language learning journey as well. If so, I also hope that you will share the ebook with your friends and acquaintances.

And, if you would like to encourage an aspiring writer like me to write more books, please do leave a review. Needless to say, your thoughts about my book would be a wonderful inspiration to write more!

Also, for more such wonderful tips and strategies to improve your language skills and communicate effectively, you can visit my official Blog: http://learnenglishwithpreeti.online/

Additionally, if you would be interested, here are a few of my other works:*(Poetry & Mystery)*